FAMOUS EXPLORERS

Daniel Rogers

Wayland

Famous people

Famous Artists
Famous Campaigners for Change
Famous Explorers
Famous Inventors
Famous Musicians
Famous Scientists

Picture acknowledgements
Ann Ronan at Image Select 16, 31, 33; Archiv fur Kunst und Geschichte, Berlin 6, 7, 8, 11, 12, 13, 14, 15, 19, 36, 41; Mary Evans Picture Library (cover), 4, 28, 30, 36, 43; Michael Holford 8, 21, 24; Hutchison Library 18,/Christina Dodwell 39,/Richard House 42 (top); Peter Newark's Western Americana 5 (lower), 20, 23, 25, 26, 27, 32, 42 (lower), 45 (left), 46; Christine Osborne 29; Topham Picture Library (cover), 5 (top), 33, 35, 37, 43, 45 (right); Julia Waterlow 40; Wayland Picture Library (cover), 22.
Cover artwork by Peter Dennis.

Series editor: Rosemary Ashley
Series designer: Malcolm Walker

First published in 1993 by
Wayland (Publishers) Limited
61 Western Road, Hove
East Sussex, BN3 1JD, England

British Library Cataloguing in Publication Data
Rogers, Daniel
  Famous Explorers. -(Famous People Series)
  I. Title II. Series
  910.922

ISBN 0-7502-0670-5

Typeset by Kudos Editorial and Design Services
Printed and bound in Italy by Rotolito Lombardo S.p.A, Milan

Contents

Introduction

Until the tenth century little was known about countries outside Europe and the Mediterranean lands. Since then, almost every part of the earth and even the moon have been explored.

The Ancient Egyptians first sailed along the African coast about 1000 BC. About AD 100, Chinese traders crossed deserts and mountains to reach India. Vikings sailed the Atlantic to North America in 986 and Portuguese seamen voyaged around Africa and across the Indian Ocean to the Far East in the 1400s. Meanwhile, Spaniards were sailing west to the Americas. Later, explorers opened up Africa, Australia and the polar regions.

Although we often say explorers 'discovered' new lands, almost everywhere they went they found people already living there. Sadly, in many cases, the explorers treated these native peoples very badly.

Marco *Polo*

Pioneer explorer

Marco Polo travelled to China from Venice, in 1271. His journey took him four years. He stayed in China for seventeen years, recording what he saw on his journeys around the empire of Kublai Khan. After returning to Italy in 1295, he wrote a book describing his travels and the wonders he had seen in China.

Marco Polo's father and uncle, Niccolò and Maffeo, were merchants in the Italian city of Venice. In 1260 they journeyed to China, and were introduced to the country's ruler, Kublai Khan. Unlike some of the earlier Chinese emperors, Kublai was keen to encourage trade and he greeted the Polo brothers warmly. Before they returned to Venice, Kublai asked them to take letters from him to the Pope in Rome.

This illustration, from a fourteenth-century manuscript, shows Marco Polo leaving Venice at the start of his journey to China in 1271.

The Polos travelled part of the return journey from China by boat. This picture shows them calling at Hormuz in the Persian Gulf. As you can see, their pack-animals are shown in the boat with them!

In 1271 the brothers again set out for China, this time taking young Marco with them. Pope Gregory X gave the party his blessing and asked them to deliver letters to Kublai Khan. Their journey to China took them through Persia (modern-day Iran and Iraq), Afghanistan, and across the deserts and mountains of Central Asia. At last, in 1275 the Polos reached Kublai Khan's summer capital at Shang-tu.

Throughout the journey, Marco Polo had written about what he saw, from the jewel markets of Persia to the large wild sheep of the Pamir mountains. (The sheep were later named *ovis poli* in his honour.) In Shang-tu, he found almost too many marvels to write about. He was especially impressed by Kublai Khan's palace, with its fabulous painted decorations showing birds, animals and plants of all descriptions.

The Polos then travelled south with Kublai to the newly built capital at Khanbalik (now

Kublai Khan, the emperor of China.

known as Beijing). Marco Polo became a favourite of Kublai Khan, who sent him on business expeditions throughout his vast empire. Kublai also asked him to bring back reports about how the people of China lived. When Marco returned to Kublai's palace after each journey, he became a kind of royal storyteller, with the task of telling the court fascinating tales about the far-flung parts of the empire.

Marco Polo stayed in China for seventeen years. By 1292, however, he was keen to return home. He persuaded Kublai to allow him to leave, and he sailed with his father and uncle from the southern city of Ch'uan-chou (modern Zaitun) to Hormuz on the Persian Gulf. They then travelled overland to the Black Sea and boarded a ship bound for Constantinople (Istanbul), finally reaching Venice in 1295.

Shortly after his return, Marco Polo joined the Venetian forces which were then at war with the rival state of Genoa. In 1296 he was captured and spent two years in prison. During that time, he wrote a book about his travels. When it was published, *The Travels of Marco Polo* described so many unknown wonders that most people refused to believe it was true. Among the marvels he wrote about were paper money, printing, water-clocks, gunpowder and coal.

Years later, as he lay dying, Marco Polo was asked if he had made up his fabulous tales of China. He replied, 'I have not told half of what I saw.' Gradually, as more and more travellers visited China and brought back their own reports, people realized that Marco Polo had indeed seen all the wonders he had described.

An old manuscript painting of Marco Polo.

Dates

1254 born in Venice, Italy
1271 sets out for China with his father and uncle
1275 they reach Kublai Khan's summer capital at Shang-tu and journey on to new capital at Khanbalik
1277-92 Marco Polo travels throughout China
1292 Polos leave China
1295 they reach Venice
1296 Marco Polo captured by Genoese
1296-98 writes account of his travels, later published as *The Travels of Marco Polo*
1324 dies in Venice

Ibn *Battuta*

Traveller in Africa and Asia

Ibn Battuta's travels began in 1325 when he made a pilgrimage to the holy city of Mecca, in Arabia. He visited all the Muslim countries of the known world and many other lands besides. He was regarded as the most widely travelled person of his time. Although some people thought the accounts he wrote about his travels were very fanciful, they have since been found to be mainly accurate.

Ibn Battuta was born in Tangier, Morocco. He came from a wealthy Muslim family and he trained to be a judge. Like all Muslims, he wanted to make a pilgrimage to Mecca, birthplace of the Prophet Muhammad and the most holy city of Islam.

In 1325, at the age of twenty-one, Ibn Battuta set out overland across north Africa. Along the way, he decided that travelling was far

An ancient Arabic painting of a camel caravan. In Ibn Battuta's time, camel caravans were used to transport goods throughout the Middle East, North Africa and parts of central Asia.

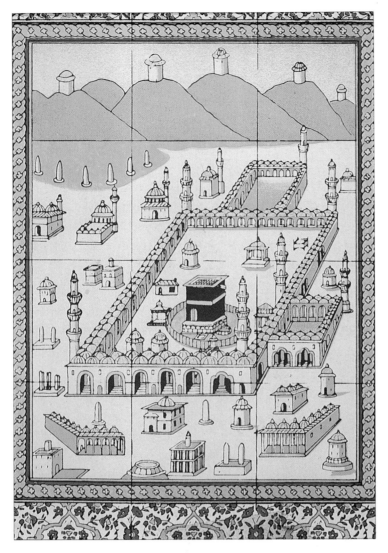

An illustration showing the holy city of Mecca. The black building in the centre of the picture is the Ka'aba – the most sacred pilgrim shrine in Islam.

more exciting than studying law. He became determined to see as much of the known world as he could, especially those lands where the people followed the religion of Islam. He made one rule for himself – that he would never travel the same road twice.

He began exploring the lands of the Middle East. After passing through Egypt he went on to Jerusalem and Damascus, where he joined a camel caravan bound for Mecca (in present-day Saudi Arabia). From there he trekked across the vast Arabian Desert and on through what is now Iraq, Iran and Turkey. After returning to Mecca, he set out again in 1330. He sailed along the southern coast of Arabia, across the Gulf of Aden and down the East African coast as far as Zanzibar, an island off present-day Tanzania.

Two years later Ibn Battuta began the most daring of all his journeys – to India. He travelled overland through Syria, across the Caucasus Mountains and into Afghanistan. At last he reached the city of Daybul, at the mouth of the great River Indus, and then travelled on to Delhi. From 1332 to 1344 he journeyed in and around India, visiting the trading city of Calicut (now Kozhikode), the Maldive Islands, Ceylon (Sri Lanka) and Chittagong (in modern-day Bangladesh).

Then he joined a trading expedition to China, before returning to Tangier in 1349.

Ibn Battuta's final expedition, in 1352, took him south across the Sahara Desert to the great African kingdom of Mali, which had never before been visited by Western travellers. He continued on to the River Niger and to the ancient Muslim city of Timbuktu. By the time he returned home to Morocco in 1353, Ibn Battuta had travelled over 120,000 km.

Dates

1304 born in Tangier, Morocco
1325 makes pilgrimage to Mecca and travels through Mesopotamia and Persia
1330 explores East African coast
1332 sets out for India
1332-44 travels in and around India
1349 returns to Tangier
1352 visits West African kingdom of Mali
1353 returns to Morocco and settles in city of Fez
c1368 dies in Fez

On his journeys around the Persian Gulf and along the east coast of Africa, Ibn Battuta travelled in boats similar to this Arab craft.

Christopher *Columbus*

Voyaging to the 'New World'

Christopher Columbus sailed across the Atlantic Ocean, hoping to find a route to the Far East. He sailed in the opposite direction to the Portuguese sailors who were voyaging around Africa, also looking for a way to the East. He reached lands never before visited by Europeans and opened the way to the 'New World'. He died without ever seeing the vast Pacific Ocean and still believing that China was only a short distance beyond South America.

Christopher Columbus was born in Genoa, Italy. He went to sea on a cargo ship at the age of fifteen. In 1476 he was shipwrecked off the coast of Portugal. He decided to settle in the country and made his way to the city of Lisbon. In 1478 he sailed to the island of Madeira on a trading voyage and he later married Dona Felipa Perestrello, who lived on one of the islands in the Madeiras group.

At that time, Portugal, backed by Prince Henry the Navigator, was sending ships and seafarers on voyages of exploration and discovery. Portuguese seamen were venturing further and further along the coast of West Africa, returning with many treasures (and slaves). Columbus made at least one voyage

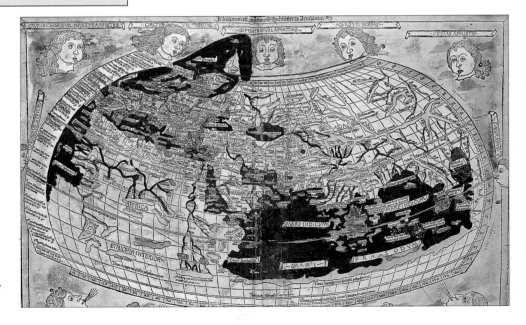

This map of the world was published in 1486. It shows how little Europeans knew about the world at that time.

Columbus's three ships, the Pinta, Santa Maria *and* Niña, *set sail across the Atlantic on 3 August 1492.*

to the Portuguese trading post at São Jorge da Mina, on the Gold Coast of West Africa.

The Portuguese hoped to find a way around Africa to the Spice Islands, in the East Indies (now called the Moluccas), and China. The valuable trade in spices and silk from these lands was controlled by Arab merchants, who transported the goods overland through Asia. Consequently, the spices and silk were extremely expensive when they finally arrived in Europe. Portuguese merchants and sailors knew that if they could find a sea route to the East they could obtain the precious goods cheaply and make their fortunes by selling them in Europe.

While the Portuguese explored further and further down the coast of Africa, Columbus had a different idea. He believed that he could reach China and Japan by sailing westward across the Atlantic Ocean. His plan was rejected by King John II of Portugal, apparently because John refused to believe that Japan existed. In 1486, Columbus took his plan to King Ferdinand and Queen Isabella of Spain. They took a long time to accept his plan but finally, on 3 August 1492, the expedition set sail from Palos, Spain. After calling at the Canary Islands for repairs, the three ships – the *Niña*, the *Pinta* and the *Santa Maria* – headed due west, out into the Atlantic.

On 12 October land was sighted. This was an island in what we now call the Bahamas. Columbus named the island San Salvador and then sailed south, reaching the island of Cuba. He was convinced that he was at the edge of Asia, and he sent men to search for the emperor of China. The *Santa Maria* was wrecked on a reef off another island, which Columbus called La Española. After leaving forty-three men there – and establishing the first European settlement in the New World – Columbus returned to Spain in triumph.

Ferdinand and Isabella were convinced that the islands Columbus had found were off the coast of Asia. They commissioned him to make a second voyage, which set sail in September 1493. On reaching La Española, Columbus found that the men he had left behind had been killed by the islanders. He formed another settlement, called Isabella, and left his brother Diego in charge while he continued to explore the region. He sailed along the southern coast of Cuba and landed on Jamaica. He returned to La Española, where he brutally put down rebellions among both the islanders and the European settlers. In June 1496 he sailed for Spain.

Right   A portrait of Christopher Columbus painted not long after his death.

Columbus and his men land on the island of San Salvador.

Ferdinand and Isabella were angry when they learned of Columbus's cruel behaviour on La Española. Nonetheless, they ordered him to make another voyage in 1498. This time he took a more southerly route than before and reached the coast of what is now Venezuela, on the South American mainland. He then turned north to La Española, which was once again in revolt. King Ferdinand and Queen Isabella sent a new governor to the settlement to restore order. The governor's first act was to arrest Columbus and ship him back to Spain in chains. Although he was released on arrival, he was in disgrace. He asked for one more chance to regain his good name and was given four ships to make a new voyage.

Columbus hoped to find a passage to the Indian Ocean between Cuba and South America, and was sure that China lay only a short distance to the north-west. He sailed along the coast of Central America and on New Year's Day 1503 he anchored off Panama. Although he did not know it, he was closer than he had ever been to the Pacific Ocean. Eventually he gave up his search and returned to Spain on 7 September 1504. Two years later he died in poverty.

Ferdinand *Magellan*

The first voyage around the world

Ferdinand Magellan sailed with five ships across the Atlantic, to find a way around South America and into the Pacific. This became the first voyage right around the world. During the voyage, the *Vittoria* travelled more than 67,500 km – half through seas that had never before been sailed by Europeans. Although he was killed before the ship returned to Spain, Magellan is given the credit for this great achievement.

Magellan served as a seaman in the Portuguese navy and spent much of his time sailing the Indian Ocean. On one of his voyages, he became the first European to land in the Philippines. Some years earlier, ships from Portugal had found a route around the southern cape of Africa to reach India and the Spice Islands, while Columbus had discovered a westward route to the Americas. Both Spain and Portugal were growing rich

An old engraving of the port of Lisbon in Portugal, as it was in the mid-sixteenth century.

14

In October 1520 Magellan found the strait that joins the Atlantic and Pacific oceans.

through their trade with the lands they had visited.

In 1513, Magellan was wrongly accused of treachery and returned to Portugal in disgrace. Realizing that he had no chance of being given the command of a ship, he did what Columbus had done and crossed the border to Spain. Shortly after he arrived, Magellan put forward a plan to King Charles V of Spain. His idea was to reach the Far East by sailing west instead of east. He was sure that there must be a way around the American continent and that China and Japan lay just beyond. He asked the king to pay for an expedition and, within two months of Magellan's arrival, Charles agreed.

On 20 September 1519, Magellan left Spain with 277 men and five ships: the *Trinidad*, the *Vittoria*, the *Santiago*, the *Concepcion* and the

San Antonio. The fleet crossed the Atlantic Ocean and sailed down the coast of South America. Magellan was searching for a narrow strait leading from the Atlantic into the Pacific. In January 1520, he thought he had found it but was disappointed to discover that the 'strait' was the mouth of a river. There were other setbacks. He had to put down a mutiny and shortly after the *Santiago* was wrecked in a storm. However, Magellan pressed on and in October he found the channel which led to the Pacific; it is still known as the Strait of Magellan.

Even though Magellan had been proved right, some of the men still wanted to return home. The crew of the *San Antonio* mutinied and sailed back to Spain, carrying with them a large part of the fleet's food. After searching for the missing ship, Magellan and his men sailed on through the strait into the Pacific Ocean in November 1520, convinced that they would reach Asia in three or four days.

But Magellan did not know, as we now know, that the Pacific is the largest ocean on Earth. The three remaining ships sailed on for many weeks without sighting land and eventually the food ran out. After ninety-eight days at sea they finally spotted an island – one of the Marianas (east of the Philippines).

A woodcut print of Magellan.

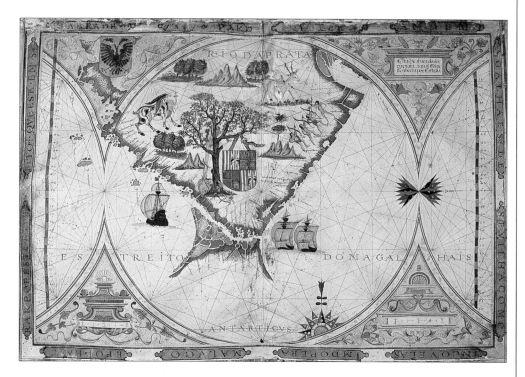

A sixteenth-century map showing the tip of South America and the Strait of Magellan.

The men went ashore to stock up with food. They set sail again and landed in the Philippines ten days later.

Sadly, Magellan was killed in a battle on one of the Philippine Islands. After this, an officer named John Carvalho sank the *Concepcion*, and the two remaining ships then headed for the Spice Islands. Carvalho loaded up the *Trinidad* with spices and other goods, but was captured by the Portuguese on his way back to Spain.

Meanwhile, on 21 February 1522, the *Vittoria* headed west under the command of Sebastián del Cano. The homeward journey took del Cano through seas controlled by the Portuguese and he dared not put ashore to get food. Many of the crew of sixty died of disease and hunger. By the time the *Vittoria* reached Spain on 6 September 1522, only eighteen men were left alive. They had completed the first circumnavigation of the globe – a brilliant feat of navigation and seamanship.

Dates

1480 born in Sabrosa, Portugal
1505 becomes seaman on voyage to India
1513 accused of treachery and returns to Portugal
1517 leaves Portugal for Spain
1519 sets out across Atlantic Ocean with five ships
1520 finds Strait of Magellan and enters Pacific Ocean
1521 killed in battle in Philippines
1522 Sebastián del Cano and eighteen survivors return to Spain on the *Vittoria*.

Francisco *de Orellana*

Voyaging down the Amazon

Franciso de Orellana joined an expedition to explore the South American rainforest to the east of the Andes mountains. When the expedition ran out of food, de Orellana and fifty men set out in a ship downriver, in search of food. They found themselves drifting down the River Amazon and finally reached the river's mouth after six months. They were the first Europeans to make the journey.

Early in the sixteenth century, Spanish invaders began to conquer and exploit the lands of South and Central America. Soldiers went in search of gold, silver and jewels, which they transported back to Spain in huge treasure ships. Among the soldiers was Francisco de Orellana. In 1535 he went on an expedition to Peru and fought with the troops led by the Spanish conqueror Francisco Pizarro. Three years later, de Orellana was

Above   A tributary of the River Amazon, flowing through dense Amazon rainforest which has changed little since de Orellana's time.

Left   A sixteenth-century painting showing South American Indians bringing gold to the Spanish soldiers who conquered them.

made governor of Guayaquil, on the Pacific coast of South America, in what is now Ecuador.

In 1541 de Orellana was appointed second-in-command of an expedition led by Pizarro's brother Gonzales. Their plan was to explore the unknown land to the east of the Andes mountains and search for new supplies of treasure. They travelled over the high mountains and down into the rainforest beyond. In almost constant rain, they hacked their way through the forest until they reached the River Coca.

The expedition had not found any treasure, and the men were exhausted and starving. Gonzales Pizarro ordered the men to build a ship, which was to be sent on ahead of the main party. De Orellana was put in command of the vessel and he set off downriver with fifty men, in search of food. On 11 February 1542 they reached the headwaters of the great Amazon River. De Orellana found food, but only enough for his own men. He decided to carry on and try to reach the Atlantic Ocean.

Drifting with the current, de Orellana and his party reached the mouth of the Amazon in August 1542. The journey took six months. Along the way the men were attacked by hostile tribes who fired poison-tipped arrows at them.

De Orellana returned to Spain late in 1542, with accounts of gold and spices, and of warlike women who reminded him of the women called 'Amazons' in ancient Greek legends. This is how the river got its name.

De Orellana was given permission to set up a colony in the lands he had travelled through and he sailed again in 1545. After a series of disasters, his ship capsized near the mouth of the Amazon and he was drowned.

Dates

c1490 born in Trujillo, Spain
1535 lands in Peru with invading Spanish army under Francisco Pizarro
1538 becomes governor of Guayaquil
1541 appointed second-in-command of expedition to explore east of the Andes mountains
1542 reaches the River Amazon and sails downstream to the Atlantic; returns in triumph to Spain
1545 begins second expedition to the Amazon
1546 drowns when his ship capsizes

This map of the Amazon was drawn forty years after de Orellana became the first European to sail down the river.

James *Cook*

Charting the world

Captain James Cook travelled to the far south and north of the Earth and sailed right around the world. He made many important discoveries about the countries and people of the South Pacific islands, Australia and New Zealand and he proved that the unknown continent *Terra Australis* did not exist. However, even Cook could not solve the problem of the Northwest Passage, which was not discovered for another two hundred years.

James Cook first went to sea at the age of eighteen, when he became an apprentice seaman working on ships that carried coal from north-east England to London. He learned a great deal about the sea and navigation, and rose to become ship's mate.

The Resolution *and* Adventure *in Tahiti during James Cook's second voyage.*

In 1755 he was offered the command of a ship but turned the offer down. Cook had decided instead to join the Royal Navy.

As before, Cook worked hard and learned quickly. He proved to be a brilliant navigator, and by 1758 he held the rank of master, which meant he was responsible to the captain for the navigation and sailing of the ship. From 1763 to 1768 he made accurate charts of the coasts of Labrador and Newfoundland in North America.

In 1768 Cook was given the command of a ship – the *Endeavour*. His first task was to sail to the Pacific island of Tahiti to observe a very rare event – the passage of the planet Venus across the Sun. But the voyage had another purpose: to find the unknown continent of *Terra Australis*, which was believed to lie somewhere in the southern Pacific Ocean.

The *Endeavour* sailed on 25 August 1768 with ninety-four men on board, including officers, scientists, servants and crew. Four months later, the ship sailed around Cape Horn, at the tip of South America, and entered the Pacific Ocean. Cook then followed a southerly course to Tahiti in an attempt to find *Terra Australis*. But he did not discover the mystery continent, and landed on Tahiti in April 1769. The scientists made their observations on 3 June and the *Endeavour* sailed again ten days later. After exploring several islands west of Tahiti, including Easter Island with its strange statues, Cook

After crashing into the coral of the Great Barrier Reef, off the eastern coast of Australia, the Endeavour *was beached and repaired.*

and his men headed south. They had orders to search for *Terra Australis* and, if they failed to find the unknown continent, to sail on to New Zealand, which had been sighted a century earlier by the Dutch explorer Abel Tasman.

No trace was found of *Terra Australis* and Cook spent six months exploring and charting the coasts of New Zealand, before heading west to Australia (then known as New Holland). He sailed up the east coast, making charts. In April 1770 the *Endeavour* crashed on to the jagged coral of the Great Barrier Reef and only narrowly avoided being sunk. When repairs were completed, Cook sailed for home and reached England on 10 July 1771.

He was soon ordered to prepare for a second voyage in search of *Terra Australis*. On 13 July 1772 the *Resolution* and the *Adventure* set sail from Plymouth, England. The ships were to sail much further south than any European vessel had ever been before. Between November 1772 and March 1775 they travelled all the way around Antarctica, although the pack-

In 1770 Cook landed in Australia and claimed the continent as a British territory.

23

ice stretching out to sea prevented them from catching sight of the frozen continent. When Cook reached home on 30 July 1775, he became the first ship's captain to sail around the world from west to east. He was able to report that there was no need to continue the search for *Terra Australis*; it did not exist.

For his third and final expedition, Cook was asked to solve another problem that had troubled navigators for many years – the question of the Northwest Passage. This route was believed to exist to the north of Canada. The English explorer Henry Hudson had failed to find it in the 1600s. The *Resolution* and the *Discovery* sailed from Plymouth on 12 July 1776. After visiting Australia, New Zealand and Tahiti, Cook landed on the Hawaiian Islands on 20 January 1778. Two weeks later he headed towards North America and began sailing up the west coast. He passed the Bering Strait – the narrow channel between North America and north-eastern Asia – but was then forced back by ice. Determined to try again the following year, Cook returned to the Hawaiian Islands. There, sadly, he was killed in a fight with the islanders.

Dates

1728 born in Marton, Yorkshire, England
1746 becomes apprentice seaman
1755 joins Royal Navy
1768 given command of expedition to Tahiti
1770 lands in New Zealand and Australia
1772-75 second expedition; sails around Antarctica and completes first west-to-east circumnavigation of the world
1776-78 third and last expedition; fails to find Northwest Passage
1778 killed in Hawaiian Islands

Meriwether Lewis and William Clark

Opening up the West

Meriwether Lewis and William Clark knew all about hunting and living in the wild. They set out with thirty men on the first expedition across the USA to the Pacific Ocean. They faced huge natural obstacles, including the Great Falls on the Missouri River and the Rocky Mountains, and suffered attacks by grizzly bears and hostile tribes of North American Indians. In spite of these difficulties the journey was a complete success.

By the middle of the eighteenth century, the north-eastern region of North America (where the original colonies had been established) was becoming overcrowded. People knew that there was a vast area of land to the west, but it had never been properly explored or settled by Europeans.

In 1801, the president of the USA, Thomas Jefferson, decided that the time had come to explore the lands west of the great Mississippi River. He appointed his private secretary, Meriwether Lewis, to lead an expedition, and Lewis chose William Clark as his second-in-command. Lewis then set about choosing

Lewis and Clark explored along the Columbia River west of the Rocky Mountains.

equipment for the mission while Clark recruited and trained the men.

On 14 May 1804, the so-called Corps of Discovery left St Louis and sailed up the Missouri River. Their route upriver took them across the vast plains of North America, where they met several tribes of North American Indians and made peace with them. By the time the freezing winter came, the Corps of Discovery had reached part of what is now the state of North Dakota. They built a log fort and waited for warmer weather.

In spring, they built a barge and carried on up the Missouri. The journey became more difficult as the river currents became stronger. When they reached a huge waterfall – known as the Great Falls – they had to travel around it and carry all their equipment overland. The next obstacle was the snow-covered Rocky Mountains which towered over them. The expedition crossed the Rockies with the help of a Shoshoni woman called Sacagewea, who was the wife of a Canadian guide who had joined their party. Sacagewea showed them a pass which led through the mountains, and told them how to reach the Columbia River that led down to the Pacific Ocean. They climbed down the western side of the Rockies and paddled down the Columbia. Finally, on

Sacagewea, a member of the Shoshoni tribe, showed Lewis and Clark the way to a mountain pass through the Rockies.

7 November 1805, they caught sight of their goal – the Pacific Ocean.

They built a fort where they could spend the winter and watch for ships passing along the coast. However, no ships came and so they were forced to make their return journey overland. They set off on 23 March 1806. Even though they knew the way, their journey home was very hard. It was made worse by the fact that the Blackfoot – one of the many North American tribes they encountered – attacked the party. They eventually reached St Louis on 23 September 1806. They had travelled over 12,000 km and had been away so long that many people thought they must have died. Lewis and Clark had done all they had set out to do: they had found a route to the West and had forged good relations with most of the native American tribes they had met. Within a few years, traders travelled along their route westward and settlers followed in their footsteps.

Dates

1770 William Clark born in Caroline, Virginia
1774 Meriwether Lewis born in Charlottesville, Virginia
1804 Lewis and Clark set off up Missouri River from St Louis, Missouri
1805 cross Rocky Mountains and reach Pacific Ocean
1806 make return journey to St Louis
1809 Lewis killed in Nashville, Tennessee
1838 Clark dies in St Louis

Lewis and Clark came across many native American tribes. Most were friendly but some, especially the Blackfoot, attacked the explorers.

Robert *Burke* and William *Wills*

Across Australia

By the late 1850s, the coastline of Australia had been well mapped, but the interior of the country was still unknown to all but the Aborigines who lived there. In 1859, the government of South Australia offered a prize to the first person to cross the continent from south to north. The following year, an expedition led by Robert Burke and William Wills left Melbourne to try to claim the prize.

The expedition party consisted of the two leaders and fifteen men. They were extremely

Robert Burke and William Wills set out to cross Australia from south to north. But they had never explored before and they did not know the country they would have to cross. The terrible heat of the desert and heavy rains in the north turned the expedition into a nightmare. Although they reached the northern coast of Australia, Burke and Wills and a third man died of starvation on the return journey. Only one man, John King, was rescued and got back to Melbourne.

Right   A dried-out river bed in the desert region north of Cooper Creek.

well equipped, with twenty-three horses and wagons, and twenty-five camels, which were taken because they are ideally suited to travelling across deserts. Unfortunately both Burke and Wills were almost entirely unfit for the task they had been given. Neither of them knew much about the country they would have to cross and they had little experience of exploration. To make matters worse, they soon proved to be poor leaders.

The expedition began well when, in August 1860, the party was cheered on its way out of Melbourne by an excited crowd. But soon quarrels broke out among the men and Burke dismissed some of them. He now decided to leave some of his party behind and pressed on, taking only Wills and three other men with him.

In the scorching heat, they travelled north and reached Cooper Creek, the half-way point of their journey, in October. Burke left one of the men, William Brahe, in charge of the remaining animals and stores. He was told to wait for three months or until the stores ran out, while Burke, Wills, Charles Gray and John King tried to reach the Gulf of Carpentaria on the north coast. A sudden change in the weather brought heavy rain that turned the ground to mud. The camels could

Left   The group of men led by Burke and Wills were cheered as they left Melbourne on 20 August 1860, at the start of their journey across Australia.

29

not move in those conditions and so Burke and Wills left the other two and continued on foot. In mid-February they finally caught sight of the sea, but their way was blocked by swamps so they decided to turn back.

The return journey was a disaster. Burke and Wills met up with Gray and King and headed for Cooper Creek. Once again, heavy rains made travelling almost impossible and the men caught a fever. When the food began to run out, the camels were shot, one by one, for their meat. Finally, Gray collapsed and died.

When the three survivors reached Cooper Creek, they found that Brahe had left just seven hours earlier. After wandering in the desert for weeks, the three men were rescued and fed by Aborigines. When they returned to Cooper Creek, they found that Brahe had arrived with a search party and, finding no signs of life, he had returned to Melbourne.

Burke, Wills and King were now completely out of food and they began to starve. Wills was the first to die, and a few days later Burke died too. John King was now the only survivor. He staggered out into the desert and was found by a group of Aborigines. They looked after him until another rescue party arrived and took him back to Melbourne.

Dates

1820 Robert Burke born in County Galway, Ireland
1833 William Wills born in Devon, England
1853 Burke emigrates to Australia
1860 expedition leaves Melbourne to cross Australia
1861 they almost reach the north coast before turning back; Burke and Wills die of starvation; only survivor, John King, rescued and taken back to Melbourne
1862 remains of Burke and Wills recovered for state funeral in Melbourne

Nearing the end of their ordeal, Burke, Wills and King struggle on without food or water.

Henry Morton *Stanley*

Explorer in Africa

Henry Stanley became famous when he found the explorer David Livingstone, who had been missing in Africa for five years. Stanley spent many years exploring Africa. He proved that Lake Victoria was the source of the River Nile. He sailed down the mighty River Congo and explored country that had never before been seen by Europeans.

Henry Morton Stanley travelled through regions of the African continent little known to Europeans at that time.

Stanley's real name was John Rowlands. He was born in Wales and spent his childhood in an orphanage. In his teens, he ran away and found work as a cabin boy on a ship bound for North America. In the USA he met a wealthy cotton merchant from New Orleans, called Henry Morton Stanley, who adopted him. Rowlands changed his name in gratitude to his adoptive father.

Young Stanley's life was very adventurous. He fought in the American Civil War (1861–65), and later joined the navy. Finally he became a journalist and worked for the *New York Herald*. In 1869, the newspaper sent him to look for the British explorer David Livingstone, who had been missing in Africa for three years. Stanley made his preparations for the trip and arrived in Zanzibar, on the east coast of Africa, at the beginning of 1871.

Later that year, Stanley left Zanzibar with two European assistants, 192 porters and a large amount of supplies. The difficult journey west took them through swamps and scrubland. On the way, Stanley fell ill with malaria and his assistants both died.

After a difficult and dangerous journey, Stanley finally found the Scottish explorer and missionary, David Livingstone. They met at Ujiji, near the shores of Lake Tanganyka on 10 November 1871.

On their journey down the River Congo, Stanley's men had to carry the expedition's boats overland through the forest, to avoid waterfalls.

Eventually, on 10 November 1871, Stanley reached the village of Ujiji (in present-day Tanzania). He was greeted by an excited crowd and then taken to meet Livingstone, who was very frail and sick. The food and medicine Stanley had brought soon restored Livingstone to good health, and the two men then set off to explore Lake Tanganyika. After they parted Stanley returned to Zanzibar. Before he left Africa, he sent Livingstone fresh supplies. Sadly, Livingstone died of fever in 1873.

Stanley's travels with Livingstone inspired him to return to Africa and he began his second expedition in 1874. He was determined to find the source of the River Nile, which flows into the Mediterranean Sea in Egypt. Some years earlier, the explorer John Hanning Speke had discovered that the Nile flows out of Lake Victoria and was convinced that the lake was the river's source, but he had no real proof. Stanley decided to solve the mystery.

He headed west and explored Lake Victoria, proving that it was indeed the source of the Nile. He then went on to explore more of Lake Tanganyika before travelling west to Nyangwe on the Lualaba River. The final stage of his journey was the most dangerous. Stanley was sure that the Lualaba flowed into the great Congo River, which reaches the sea at

The densely forested banks of the River Congo (now called the Zaire) remain an inhospitable region for most Europeans.

Boma on Africa's west coast. He and his companions decided to sail down the Lualaba to prove this.

On their journey downriver the party were frequently attacked by warrior tribes, some of whom were cannibals. Finally in August 1877 Stanley reached Boma. He had explored the last of Africa's great rivers, but only 114 members of his original party of 356 remained. The rest had either died or deserted. In 1887 Stanley returned to Africa for his last expedition. He went to Sudan to rescue an explorer named Emin Pasha who had become cut off from the outside world. Stanley travelled up the River Congo with a team of over 600 men. The party then had to hack their way through dense rainforest to the shores of Lake Albert, in present-day Zaire. Stanley met Emin Pasha in April 1888 and discovered that he did not really need rescuing, which made his mission something of a flop! Nonetheless, Stanley returned to England in triumph.

Dates

1841 Born John Rowlands in Wales

1859 adopted by Henry Stanley in New Orleans, USA; changes his name to Henry Morton Stanley

1871-72 first expedition to Africa; finds David Livingstone and explores Lake Tanganyika

1874-77 second expedition; explores Lake Victoria and proves it is source of River Nile; sails down River Congo

1887-88 final expedition, to rescue Emin Pasha

1904 dies in Surrey, England

Mary *Kingsley*

African travels

> Mary Kingsley spent a quiet childhood in London, England. When she was thirty-one she travelled to south-west Africa, to the country now called Angola. This was a very unusual thing for a woman to do in the 1890s. She made two journeys in West Africa, and lived happily among the local tribespeople. During her stays in Africa she learned a great deal about the land, its plants and animals, and about the people and their culture.

A portrait of Mary Kingsley before she set out on her first journey to Africa.

Mary Kingsley's early life was very quiet. She was born in London and, like most wealthy girls living in the reign of Queen Victoria, she spent most of her time at home. Her father was an explorer and was often abroad on expeditions, and Mary looked after her mother while he was away. Although she never went to school and had very little education, Mary became a keen reader and was fascinated by her father's library of scientific and geographical books.

In 1892 Mary's parents died, and she was free to do what she liked. Having learned a

Gabon in West Africa, which Mary Kingsley visited when she made her second African journey.

great deal about Africa from her father's books, she was determined to see it for herself. A year later she boarded a ship bound for the part of south-west Africa now called Angola.

On arrival, after making final preparations, Mary Kingsley and a small team of African porters set off inland. They followed the course of the River Congo upstream. She found that she loved being in Africa and was fascinated by its forests and plains, and its wildlife and people. She returned home to England in 1894 with many specimens of beetles and river fish, which she took to the Natural History Museum in London.

However, Mary Kingsley was restless in England and could hardly wait to go back to Africa. The following year she began her second expedition. This time she went to a different part of West Africa – Gabon – and travelled up the River Ogooué. Among the people she met were members of the Fang, a tribe of cannibals. Far from being afraid, Mary lived among them for several months and bartered with them to obtain food. She learned how to paddle a canoe in the fast-flowing waters of the Ogooué and collected many rare specimens of fish.

When she returned to England, Mary wrote *Travels in West Africa*, which was based on the diaries she had kept while on her journeys. When the book was published in 1899 it became a bestseller. The following year, Mary travelled to South Africa to nurse soldiers wounded in the Boer War. While she was there, she caught a fever and died.

Dates

1862 born in Islington, London
1892 both her parents die
1893-94 first expedition to West Africa; travels up River Congo and collects specimens of rare beetles and fish
1895 second expedition; travels up River Ogooué in Gabon
1899 *Travels in West Africa* published and becomes a bestseller
1900 dies of fever in South Africa

The lives of the riverside peoples of West Africa have changed little since Mary Kingsley lived among them in the nineteenth century.

Sven *Hedin*

Traveller to Tibet and western China

Sven Hedin spent many years travelling in the mountains and deserts of central Asia, especially in the little-known country of Tibet. He tried to visit the forbidden city of Lhasa, disguised as a monk, but was caught and sent away. Later he returned to Tibet and made maps of the country. He made many important discoveries about the history of Tibet and north-west China.

A photograph of Sven Hedin taken on his travels in central Asia.

From the age of fifteen, Sven Hedin knew that he wanted to become an explorer. To prepare himself he studied map-making and learned seven languages. The part of the world that excited him most was central Asia, and especially the country of Tibet. Even a hundred years ago, very few Europeans had travelled to Tibet and Hedin longed to find out more about this mysterious land.

Hedin's travels began in 1885, when he went from his home in Stockholm, Sweden, to Persia (present-day Iran and Iraq) to work as a teacher. Five years later he began exploring the remote areas of central Asia. Between 1890 and 1908, he was constantly travelling in Tibet, the Himalaya Mountains and the Taklamakan Desert, north of Tibet.

In 1894 Hedin made his first journey to the borders of Tibet with two other men. They made their way through high mountain passes and then set out across the Taklamakan Desert. This journey almost ended in disaster. Hedin's party ran out of water and one man died. Hedin and his remaining companion then struggled on for three days through the scorching heat. Finally, almost dead from thirst, they found a shallow pool of water and were saved.

Three years later, Hedin returned to the Taklamakan. This time he went in winter and travelled by river. But the boat became frozen in the ice and the party continued on foot. They found the remains of the long-lost city of Lou-lan, which had once been an important centre along the Silk Road from China.

In 1900 and 1901, Hedin made two attempts to reach the city of Lhasa, the capital of Tibet. European travellers were forbidden to enter the city, so Hedin disguised himself as a Buddhist monk. However, he was discovered by Tibetan troops before he could enter Lhasa and was sent back to the border.

The Taklamakan Desert, where Hedin almost died of thirst on his first attempt to reach Tibet in 1894.

In 1906 Hedin crossed into Tibet again. He spent the next two years exploring its mountains and rivers, and made the first detailed map of the country. In 1907 he found the source of the mighty River Indus, which flows into the sea in Pakistan. He was given a hero's welcome when he returned home to Sweden.

Hedin's last adventures were between 1927 and 1933, when he led a scientific expedition to north-west China. While he was there he made important archaeological and historical findings and collected thousands of interesting objects, which are now kept at the Sven Hedin Foundation in Stockholm.

Dates

1865 born in Stockholm, Sweden
1885 becomes teacher in Persia
1890 begins travels in central Asia
1894 explores borders of Tibet and crosses Taklamakan Desert
1898 crosses Taklamakan Desert again; discovers lost city of Lou-lan
1900-1901 makes two unsuccessful attempts to enter forbidden city of Lhasa
1906-1908 explores Tibet and makes first detailed map
1927-33 leads scientific expedition to China
1952 dies in Stockholm

Roald *Amundsen*

Polar explorer

As a young man, Amundsen was fascinated by accounts he read of the explorers who were trying to reach the North Pole. In 1886 an American, Robert Peary, began a series of expeditions across Greenland, each one taking him closer to the Pole. Then, between 1893 and 1896, one of Amundsen's fellow Norwegians, Fridtjof Nansen, tried and failed to get there. Amundsen was determined that he too would be a polar explorer.

In 1897 he joined an expedition to the Antarctic, although he did not travel far inland. Six years later Amundsen took charge of an expedition to the Arctic. After sailing to the edge of the pack-ice, he and his team travelled by dog-sled and located the exact position of the North Magnetic Pole. Returning to his ship, Amundsen sailed through the Bering Strait and landed in Alaska. In doing so, he became the first person to navigate the Northwest Passage.

Roald Amundsen became the most successful of all the polar explorers. He commanded the first ship to navigate the Northwest Passage. He led the first party to reach the South Pole, and he was the first to travel to both Poles. He made sure that his expeditions were properly equipped and that the men were used to living and travelling in snow and ice.

Roald Amundsen photographed on an Arctic expedition.

Having travelled in both the Arctic and the Antarctic, Amundsen knew how to survive in freezing conditions. He decided that on his next expedition he would attempt to reach the North Pole. However, in 1909 he learned that Robert Peary had claimed to have reached it already, so Amundsen changed his mind and headed for Antarctica and the South Pole. He knew that he was entering a race, because the English explorer Robert Scott was also leading an expedition to the Pole.

Above Sunset over the frozen continent of Antarctica.

In January 1911, Amundsen's team landed in the Bay of Whales, Antarctica. Their base there was 97 km closer to the South Pole than Scott's. When the Antarctic spring arrived, Amundsen and four of his men set out to make a dash for the Pole. They were able to travel much faster than Scott's party because they

used sleds pulled by dogs rather than by horses. (Scott's horses eventually became stuck in the snow and had to be shot, leaving the men to pull the sleds themselves.) On 14 December 1911, Amundsen and his men reached the South Pole, thirty-five days before Scott's party. While Amundsen's group returned safely to their base, Scott and all his companions died on their return journey from the Pole.

In 1918 Amundsen returned to the Arctic and led an expedition that sailed through the Northeast Passage. This was a route to the north of Russia that navigators had been trying to find for centuries. His final achievement was to fly over the North Pole in an airship, the *Norge*, in 1926. Two years later, Amundsen disappeared in the Arctic. He lost his life attempting to rescue the pilot of another airship which had crashed in the ice.

Dates

1872 Roald Amundsen born in Borge, Norway
1897-99 joins expedition to the Antarctic
1903-1906 locates position of North Magnetic Pole; becomes first person to navigate Northwest Passage
1910 begins expedition to South Pole
1911 becomes first person to reach South Pole
1918-20 leads expedition through Northeast Passage
1926 flies over North Pole in airship *Norge*
1928 Amundsen disappears in the Arctic while searching for missing pilot

Left   On their way to the South Pole, members of Amundsen's party check their position in the frozen Antarctic wastes.

Right   Amundsen and his men raised the Norwegian flag at the South Pole on 14 December 1911. They were the first people ever to set foot there.

Neil *Armstrong*

First man on the moon

Three years after his first space flight, Neil Armstrong was chosen to lead the most important of the USA's Apollo space missions. On 20 July 1969 he stepped from the *Eagle* lunar module to become the first person ever to walk on the moon. Although he and his fellow astronaut, 'Buzz' Aldrin, stayed there for less than a day, the moon landing was one of the world's greatest feats of exploration.

Neil Armstrong was born in Wapakoneta, Ohio, in the USA. He went to school and university, and then joined the United States Air Force. After serving as a fighter pilot during the Korean War (1950-53), he became a test pilot. His job was to fly and test the performance of new aircraft that were being developed.

The most important period of Armstrong's life began in 1962. In that year he was selected to become an astronaut on the USA's space programme. After a great deal of training, he went into space for the first time in 1966, as commander of the Gemini 8 mission. While in orbit around the Earth, Gemini 8 joined up with another spacecraft, called *Agena*, before returning to splash down in the Pacific Ocean.

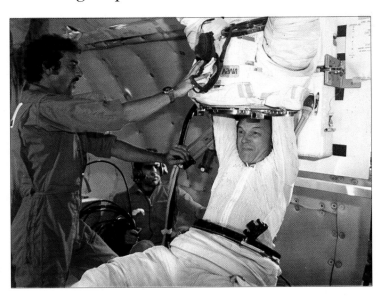

An American astronaut in training.

The purpose of this and other Gemini flights was to develop the technology that would be needed to achieve the USA's main goal in space – to land a manned spacecraft on the moon. The moon programme, codenamed Apollo, began in 1967. The first manned spacecraft to go into orbit around the moon was Apollo VIII in December 1968. The vital mission to land men on the moon's surface began on 16 July 1969, when Apollo XI was launched with Armstrong in command.

Armstrong and his fellow crew members, Edwin 'Buzz' Aldrin and Michael Collins, were launched into space by a massive Saturn

Above   The launch of the Apollo XI mission on 16 July 1969.

Right   Filmed by Armstrong, 'Buzz' Aldrin climbs down from the lunar module Eagle *on to the surface of the moon.*

V rocket and their command module went into orbit around the moon. Armstrong and Aldrin then entered the lunar module *Eagle*, which separated from the command module, and dropped towards the moon. Armstrong guided the craft to a safe landing in an area of the moon called the Sea of Tranquility. On Sunday 20 July 1969, Armstrong climbed out of the *Eagle* and became the first person to walk on the moon. As he stepped on to the surface of the moon, his first words, 'One small step for man; one giant leap for mankind', became instantly famous.

After less than twenty-four hours, *Eagle* lifted off from the moon to rejoin the command module and return to Earth. Armstrong and Aldrin took back samples of rock and soil from the surface of the moon. These samples, and those collected on later moon landings, have been studied by scientists all over the world and have provided clues about how the moon was formed millions of years ago.

Dates

1930 born in Wapakoneta, Ohio, USA
1962 begins training as an astronaut in USA's space programme
1966 commands Gemini 8 mission; achieves first docking manoeuvre with another spacecraft
1969 commands Apollo XI mission; becomes first person to walk on the moon
1971-79 teaches aerospace engineering at Cincinatti University, USA

Before returning to Earth, Neil Armstrong planted a US flag on the moon.

Glossary

Aborigines The original people living in Australia.

Bartered Goods exchanged without payment of money.

Charts Maps of the sea.

Circumnavigation Travelling all the way around something, especially the world.

Dog-sled A sled pulled by dogs, usually huskies. Dog-sleds were used to transport people and supplies across snow and ice in the regions of the Arctic and Antarctic.

Headwaters Streams that join a river near its source.

Islam The religion taught by the Prophet Muhammad.

Malaria A disease that is transmitted by the bite of a mosquito.

Mecca The birthplace of the Prophet Muhammad in Saudi Arabia, which Muslim pilgrims visit. It is the holiest place in Islam.

Merchant A person who makes his or her living by buying and selling goods.

Muslim Someone who follows the religion of Islam.

Mutiny The rebellion of seamen against their officers.

Pilgrimage A journey to a holy place.

Silk Road The route that was used long ago by merchants bringing valuable silk from China to Europe.

Source The point at which a river starts.

Strait A narrow channel linking two large areas of sea.

Trade Buying, selling or exchanging goods.

Books to read

Explorers by Tim Healey (Macdonald Educational, 1980)

The First Men on the Moon by Tim Furniss (Wayland, 1988)

The First Voyage Around the World by Roger Coote (Wayland, 1989)

The Race to the South Pole by Rupert Matthews (Wayland, 1989)

The Travels of Marco Polo by Mark Rosen (Wayland, 1988)

Twenty Names in Exploration by Alan Blackwood (Wayland, 1989)

The Usborne Book of Explorers by Felicity Everett and Struan Reid (Usborne, 1991)

The Voyage of Columbus by Rupert Matthews (Wayland, 1989)

The Voyages of Captain Cook by Richard Humble (Franklin Watts, 1990)

Index